You left your Paw Prints on my heart

A dog's home is in your ♥

You left your
Paw Prints
on my heart
A dog's home is in your ♥

LESLIE YERKES
RANDY MARTIN

Lost Dog
BOOKS
Storytellers of Trust and Love

BRATENAHL OH 44108

Lost Dog Books, LLC
10000 Lakeshore Boulevard
Cleveland OH 44108

ORDERING INFORMATION
This book is available for purchase in quantity

PRINTED IN THE UNITED STATES OF AMERICA

ISBN: 978-1-7349335-3-6
ISBN: 978-1-7349335-4-3 (Ebook)

FIRST EDITION
24 23 22 21 20   10 9 8 7 6 5 4 3 2 1
Library of Congress Control Number 2024906056

Produced and designed by Randy Martin
martinDESIGN.info 38632

Dedication

To the individuals and groups who are devoted to the rescue, rehabilitation, fostering, and adoption of dogs, cats, and other animals.

"May we all be as good people as our dogs already think we are."

Table of Contents

Big Boy's first day home.

Prologue

I WAS THINKING ABOUT how we met seven years ago on Labor Day. Back then, I didn't think of it as a lucky day or anything. But now? Now I do. I know it was lucky for me — and it certainly was for you. Buddha Bear thinks it was. And I think CoCo did, too. I know we all missed her after she went over the Rainbow Bridge. Without her running away like she did, we would never have met. And I wouldn't be writing this letter to you. But she did. And I am. If I can just finish it, at least.

So. When Officer Ryan took us to that field where you were living — I guess you could call it living, although it wasn't much more than just staying alive. Anywho, when Buddha Bear and I looked through the fence at you, I told Officer Ryan, "That's not CoCo. This dog is a really big boy." You were big, but you were just skin and bones on a beautiful body. I knew I had to do something about that.

Once we got permission from the guard at the factory to walk into the field where you were, Buddha Bear and me would bring you roasted chicken my mom made. I know you loved it even though you wouldn't let us get close to you. You remember? We'd back up a step and you'd move closer a step? Until you got close enough to that wonderful smell that you could make a dash for it, grab it, and move back to where you started, and lie down gulping bite after bite, without ever taking your eyes off of us. In the beginning, you never came closer to us than 50 feet.

When you were done eating the chicken that first time, without even thinking I called out to you, "I'll come back every day until you decide you want to come home with us." If that sounded like a promise, well, I guess it was. So I kept it.

FOR TWO MONTHS. In the heat, in the rain, and in the snow, and everything in between. We were there with you. And I think because I was keeping my promise, you started to trust us. You must have started to look forward to our visits because every time we came, you'd be closer and closer to the gate. We were sure you were looking forward to our visits. Certainly you were looking forward to the food and water we'd bring, even though most of the time it wasn't chicken. But it WAS good-tasting dog food from a can, wasn't it?

FINALLY, YOU LET ME put a collar on your neck and you came home with us. That wasn't easy or quick, but it happened. I like to think it was more than just trust. I think it was love. I think you loved us with all of your heart. In fact, I'm certain you did. Thanks for loving us like we loved you.

After a while in your new home, your bad dreams faded away.

When Grandma Betsi came to live with us that first year, you and Buddha Bear sat beside her like bookends. I think you were making sure that nothing bad could come sneaking up on her. And you boys did really good because nothing bad ever did. And when it was time for Grandma Betsi to make her way over her bridge, we were all sad for awhile. But all three of you, and me, too, I guess, made each of our lives better when we were all together. We taught each other great lessons about love and trust. And as Grandma used to say, we "Lived Large."

I wonder now if she knew that the hole she left would be large, too. I think she did. She was pretty smart, you know.

And you, Big Boy, you were brave and loving until your end came. I had no idea before that happened that dogs could get cancer, too. But they can.

I know you didn't want to leave us. But when the time came, you did.

WITH YOUR EYES LOCKED on mine, and your head in my lap, you left us to live with another big hole in our hearts. But in spite of the sadness, our lives were much better knowing you and sharing the love we had for each one of us. The whole family. Labor Day weekend will always be your weekend. Thank you for coming into our lives, sharing your journey with us, and leaving us better people.

I LOVED YOU WHEN I SAID HELLO, and I love you even more, now that we've said goodbye.

My Big Boy Memory.

You left your

Paw Prints
on my heart

A dog's home is in your ♥

Big Boys Car Ride Home.

Chapter One

The Second Beginning: Big Boy Moves In

WHENEVER I TELL THIS STORY, I always make sure to say that it started with a promise — a promise kept. One Labor Day weekend, seven years ago, me and my dog Buddha Bear were looking for Miss Monica's lost dog, CoCo. We never actually found her, but what we did find was this huge dog living wild in the back lot of a construction company near my family's house. I know that some of you didn't know any of this. But that's how it was.

FOR NEARLY TWO MONTHS, or maybe a few days more, Buddha Bear and I would take food and water out to the back lot and try to make friends with that wild dog. From the first time we saw him, Buddha Bear and me started to call him Big Boy and the name stayed with him. Eventually, just before Halloween that year, Big Boy came home with us and wound up staying with both of us, and my entire family.

BACK THEN, MY SISTER ANNE was in third grade, and my brother Jimmy was a Junior in high school. I was in 7th grade. Today, Anne is a freshman in high school, Jimmy is a Junior Lieutenant in the Marines, and I'm finishing up my first year in college. Oh, yeah. I almost forgot. Back then, everyone called me Beej. But since Grandma died, my mom wanted to honor her mother so she asked me if I would be okay with using my real name, Betsi Jane. I was fine with that. In fact, I really like being called Betsi Jane. I never could see one day being called "Grandma Beej." So, Betsi Jane is my new name. And it IS an honor, and I'm proud to be named after my grandmother. I miss her a lot, but . . . well, I guess that's part of this story.

. . .

THE FIRST MONTHS THAT BIG BOY came to live with us were not easy — for either of us. He wasn't used to living with people and he didn't know exactly what to do. And we (but mostly me) were almost overwhelmed by all the details we had to show him more than once. But luckily for him — and all of us — he was eager to learn and to put new things into his life. Now, that might sound like a pain, but it was actually fun. For me, at least. And I really think Big Boy must have been feeling a sense of accomplishment. Or whatever that's called in dog talk. But I have to say, fun or not, it was a time I'll never forget.

Something that had never really occurred to me was that Big Boy not only had to learn about what humans expected from him, but he also had to learn dog language and behavior. Living by himself in that field, he had no one to teach him, no one to watch, nor anyone even to talk to. Dogs do talk, you know. When you're around them long enough you learn to speak enough dog to get them to understand you. Even if sometimes you don't exactly understand them. It's not always a two-way street, I guess.

BUT AGAIN, I HAVE TO SAY we were all lucky because we had a secret weapon — Buddha Bear! Buddha Bear not only showed Big Boy where the sacred pee spot was, he taught him to be a good dog. He taught him how to sit and wait (boy, that was a tough one!), to walk alongside of me and not in front, and how to play friendly and not take it up to the next level. You know, the one that looks like they're one bad step away from turning fun into rough stuff? Buddha Bear even had to teach him how and when to sleep. See, when you live in the wild, you sleep in the daytime and move about in the nighttime. It's safer that way. But, when you live with humans, well, you know what I mean. Everything is backwards.

BUT BUDDHA BEAR WAS A great teacher. So patient. Such a good example of being good. Big Boy had no idea how good a teacher he had. But it paid off. We no longer had one good dog. Now we had two!

Of course, I had to do some teaching and training, too. Most of what I had to do was show Big Boy how to get along with people, something with which he had absolutely no experience. The experience Big Boy actually had with other people was something the vet helped us understand.

THE FIRST WEEK AFTER BUDDHA BEAR showed Big Boy around our house and yard, we had Dr. Terry, our vet, come to the house to do a quick check to see if Big Boy was okay.

"Well, I think he's in remarkably good condition for living all alone like he was. But to be sure, now that he knows me, I'd like you to bring him into the clinic so we can take some X-rays. Okay?"

"Okay doc, we can do that. Can't we, mom?"

Of course Mom said it was fine. A few days later, Mom said, "Betsi Jane, I think today would be a good time to take Big Boy to Dr. Terry's clinic so he can do those X-rays he wanted to take. Just to see if we might be missing something."

"Okay, Mom. I think that's a good idea. Can you drive us or should I ask Jimmy?"

"I'll be glad to do it but maybe you should ask Jimmy, anyway. Who knows? He might think it would be fun."

"FUN?" Jimmy said from the other room. "FUN? Well. It might be. Sure, I'll drive. But you have to set it up. Okay, Mom?"

"I wouldn't have it any other way."

So the following Tuesday, Jimmy helped me try to drag Big Boy into the car.

THE VERY FIRST TIME THAT Buddha Bear, Jimmy, and me tried to get Big Boy into Jimmy's car to bring him home from the field, it took us more than an hour. He just wouldn't budge and he was far too heavy — and strong — to move. We had to coax him, sing to him — well I did, at least — and bribe him with food. Finally, it took Buddha Bear getting in the car first to convince Big Boy it would be alright. And that it really was safe. Today, Big Boy LOVES riding in the car. I think he'd sit in the car all day just in the driveway if we'd let him! But back then, he still had to be, shall we say, persuaded? And it wasn't fun.

DR. TERRY IS SO GOOD WITH DOGS, even Big Boy let him poke and prod and take his X-ray pictures. And it was a good thing he did, because what he saw explained a lot about Big Boy.

"If you look here," Dr. Terry said, pointing to Big Boy's ribs on the X-ray, "you can see that at sometime he had a bunch of broken ribs. And here, one of his back legs was pretty badly broken. It's actually surprising Big Boy doesn't have a serious limp. Injuries like that can stay with a dog for years and cause all kinds of problems. But all-in-all he looks to have weathered that storm."

"How did he get the broken bones?" I asked.

"Can't tell for sure, but when you factor in that he was living by himself in a field, and kept away from people. . . and he seems to be more afraid of men than of women, I'd say he had a man for an owner who likely beat him. May even have caused the broken bones. He should be all right now, but all of you should keep an eye out whenever Big Boy's around people he doesn't know, especially men. I think the treatment he must have gotten from his previous owner taught Big Boy that men could be a danger to him. But if you all, and that includes Buddha Bear, continue to show him love, I think he'll turn out okay. I understand you're pretty sure you're going to keep him. Is that right?"

"You bet, doc. I promised to take care of him and you know I keep my promises."

"Indeed you do, young lady. Big Boy is going to be one lucky — and healthy — dog thanks to you and your family."

"Don't forget about Buddha Bear, doc. He's really the star here."

Buddha Bear
The Star.

Chapter Two

The First Year

TRAINING BIG BOY WAS MY JOB. No one really asked if they could or should help, but if they had I would have said something like, "Thanks, but this is something I should do and something that I want to do. But I appreciate your offer. And thanks for letting me make Big Boy's life even better."

You don't think that sounds too smarmy, do you?

Now, I don't want you to get the idea that I do everything that has to do be done when it comes to the dogs, 'cause I don't. And couldn't, even if I'd wanted to. We're a family and we do things like a team. And I don't mean a dog team. I mean we each have our skills and that's what we do. Mom organizes and I get it done. Jimmy gives me grief. Well, someone has to. And believe me, he's the best at it. I think it's because of all the practice he gets.

One of the things that Dad did was hire Miss Jennifer Hillman to help me with the training. When you're starting to do something you've never done before, you simply don't have any idea what to do now or what to do next. Miss Jennifer is the expert in dog training and she helped me to understand not only what I had to do but why. She said knowing why you do something makes it easier to make it happen the best way. Like for Big Boy, one of the things I had to do was train him to not resist when it was time for him and Buddha Bear to get in the car. Miss Jennifer could see what a difficult time I was having getting Big Boy in — he's 150 pounds of *I'll do what I want* and there's no way you can push him to do anything else. I mean that. You can't push him. He's too big and strong.

So Miss Jennifer coached me to find a way to make it seem like getting in the car was his idea. And that's when I said — and I have no idea why I decided to say this, I just did — "Buddha Bear. In the car."

And once Buddha Bear jumped in and looked back, Big Boy just gave a deep sigh and jumped in, knocking Buddha Bear to the other side of the back seat. And then they both looked at me, their tongues hanging out as they panted, as if to say, "OK, we're in. Aren't you going to get in, too?"

You just gotta love them, don't you?

Maybe the most important thing Miss Hillman taught me — after how to get them into the car — was why Buddha Bear was looking so unhappy.

"I don't think Buddha Bear's unhappy, Betsi Jane. I think he might be in pain.

"Big Boy is 150 pounds of muscle and Buddha Bear is only 75 pounds, so when they wrestle and crash into each other, I think Buddha Bear is getting the worst of it and I'm sure his pain is coming from his joints."

As her words moved through my ears and into my brain, they made my eyes bug out and my mouth drop open — I bet you didn't know that it's words that cause those reactions in people, but it's true (I think) — and I said, with a slight stutter, "So w-w-what should we do?"

"Well, there's nothing you can do, nor should want to do, about them playing, shall we say, ener-getically? They're young dogs and they want and need to play. Even though Buddha Bear is only half the weight of Big Boy, he is twice as fast, and if you watch, you can see Buddha Bear out-running and dancing around Big Boy. And that tires Big Boy out which slows him down even more and that makes their crashes less painful for Buddha Bear."

I was amazed. I'd watched the two of them play and I never ever thought of anything like what Miss Jennifer had said, but I knew she was right. "So, that's all we can do? Let them get tired?"

"Well, no. That's a great start, but Buddha Bear is obviously getting a physical pounding. So, what I rec-ommend — if your mom and dad agree — is to take them both to Dr. Dave the Animal Chiropractor."

And so it started. After Mom and Dad agreed, which they seemed to do pretty easily — once they got over the idea of their actually being someone who was an animal chiropractor — we went at least once a month. Sometimes more often if the dogs had been horsing around pretty hard. (Or should that be 'dogging' around? Ha!) All of that Big Boy Training paid off as he and Buddha Bear readily jumped into Mom's car once I said "Dr. Dave." And when they got into his room, when it was their turn, they each jumped up onto his table to let him adjust their neck, head, spine, and legs. I wish you could have seen the look of calm on their faces when their turn was finished. And all the way home. And for several days later.

. . .

"OKAY, STAR." I SAID TO BUDDHA BEAR. "Time for you and Big Boy to go outside and have a good romp. I'll be out in a little bit, but first I gotta talk to Mom."

So, I let them out and stood at the screen door for a few minutes, watching the two of them take turns chasing each other around the yard. Our yard is huge, especially for a city lot. Dad says we have almost a half acre, which is why he's always telling Mom we really should buy a self-propelled lawn mower. Actually, I think what he really wants is one of those riding mowers, but that's another story.

As I started to turn to Mom, she called out to me from her crafts room. I don't know how moms can do that kind of thing where they seem to know what you're going to do or say before you even do. But I know my mom seems to do it all the time. Just like what she did just then.

"I thought you were going to talk to me, Betsi Jane."

"I'm coming, Mom."

"Well, hurry up. I have to go to the grocery. We need some more dog food. And something for our dinner, too, I guess. I've never seen such a hungry group of people. And dogs, of course."

Taking care of us got a touch more demanding for Mom once Big Boy became part of our family. But I know she doesn't regret a minute of our decision. Well, maybe it was mostly MY decision, but I know Mom was definitely in favor of it.

"What's on your mind, Betsi Jane?" She didn't look up from whatever she was making, she just kept on sewing and waiting for me to talk. Which I did.

"You know how Miss Jennifer told me that she didn't think that Buddha Bear was unhappy but that maybe it was a sign of pain?"

"I do, dear. And so?"

"Well, I think maybe we should schedule a vet appointment with Dr. Terry just to see what he thinks. What do you think about that?"

"Great idea. In two minutes, just before I go shopping, I'll call his office and schedule one. Is any time okay with your schedule?"

"Mommmm! You know I'm always available."

"Yeah, well, I wasn't sure if you'd gotten a job, yet. One I didn't know about."

"Like training Big Boy isn't a full-time job? Give me a break."

Mom looked at me like she thought I had something more to say. At least that I ought to have something more to say. Something important. So I took a deep breath and said, "OK. Next week, I'll look for something I can do — if I can find a job that still lets me keep up my training."

I knew things could go downhill really fast, here, if I wasn't quick about making the next thing happen.

"I gotta go, too. Big Boy and Buddha Bear are waiting for dog-lesson number 27 and I don't want to keep them uh, waiting for me."

As I turned and hustled toward the screen door, I thought I heard Mom say something that sounded like, "Lesson 27? Like, really?" Or something like that. Like really.

. . .

"BETSI JANE, DON'T FORGET TODAY IS Buddha Bear's appointment with Dr. Terry. We have to leave at 12:30 so don't get lost, playing with your dogs."

"OK, Mom. We'll be ready. Speaking of 'we,' do you think we should take Big Boy, too? It's not really his appointment."

Mom didn't miss a beat. "Of course. Big Boy would be upset if he had to stay at home alone. I'm not sure Big Boy could spend a minute without Buddha Bear by his side."

"Yeah, you're right. It's comforting to have a real star next to you all the time, I guess."

WHEN WE PULLED UP TO THE VET, Big Boy was slow to get out, even though he was closest to the door. But after Buddha Bear barreled past him and jumped to the ground, Big Boy was gone like a shot.

"Let's get Big Boy inside," I said. "Buddha Bear, here." And that was all it took.

BOTH DOGS LOOK GREAT. You're taking good care of them," Doc Terry said. "I don't see any damage to Buddha Bear. He must be pretty resilient. And remarkably, Big Boy still shows no signs of ongoing problems from all his broken bones. Just keep up what you're doing. They could outlive both of us."

If only we'd known.

Buddha Bear and Big Boy, dashing and crashing.

Chapter Three

We Rescue Grandma

TAKING CARE OF ONE DOG is never easy. Even with a dog like Buddha Bear who is smart, observant, caring, and hungry. Yeah, I said hungry. Buddha Bear is a big dog. Clearly not in Big Boy's league, but still very big and very hungry. Coco, the next-door dog who got lost and was the reason we have Big Boy, ate like a cat. Small bites. Walk away. Come back. East slowly. Buddha Bear, though, would — you should pardon the phrase — wolf down his food as if he thought it was going to jump out of his dish and hightail it to the far reaches of, uh, well, somewhere. It seemed like he was always in a race with some unseen Dog-Food-Stealer who would dash in and devour his dinner if it weren't being eaten at full speed by Buddha Bear. Fortunately, Buddha Bear was a really fast dog, so his food always got safely into his stomach before it could be disappeared by his personal DFS nemesis. That's Dog-Food-Stealing, just so you know. It drives Mom crazy when I TIA — Talk In Initials. But I love it.

Anyway, if you think one dog is hard to take care of, try two. And when one of them is the size and temperament of Big Boy? You better know it's no way easy.

If you'd let him, Big Boy would eat twice as much as Buddha Bear in the same amount of time. Or maybe even quicker. I can't imagine ME trying to eat the size bites Big Boy can consume. It's a new definition of huge. But, I digress. IMS.

Feeding dogs is only part of what you have to do to take care of them. They need water. They need pee breaks, poop breaks, toys to play with, toys that have to be cleaned up, running time, licking time, hugging time, training time, talking time, and all kinds of time. And when you add up all those 'times' they need, you discover that if you're not careful, you'll spend all of YOUR time on them. And while it's true that dogs give you lots of love in exchange for your time, sometimes you just need them to take a time out so you can spend some time on yourself.

THERE'S ANOTHER THING ABOUT DOGS and time. They always know when it's time to eat. Yeah, I know. It's ALWAYS time for dogs to eat. But I'm talking about what time of day they get their evening feed. They know. They can tell. Well, almost. It seems that the time that they want to eat is always an hour BEFORE the time you want to feed them. So, what I wonder is, if you you were to honor THEIR time, would they eventually wind up eating dinner for breakfast? Of course they would and then they'd be hungry again at dinner. WK? (Okay, I'll stop!)

I MENTIONED TEMPERAMENT. And that Big Boy and Buddha Bear were different in that sense. Which isn't really surprising, if you think about it. I mean, look at me and Jimmy. Jimmy eats like the dogs, he sleeps like them, and he needs attention like they do. Me? I'm the kind of girl who can take care of herself, but who also finds that very same self lost in some project that takes care of others. I mean, isn't that exactly how I wound up taking care of two dogs? (And sometimes my brother?)

BUT BACK TO DOG TEMPERAMENTS. Buddha Bear is a watcher. He sits back and analyzes the situation. He lets Big Boy jump in first and then, when he's ready, Buddha Bear shows him how it's done. Big Boy is a smiler; Buddha Bear never smiles. He's friendly, he just doesn't show it. Big Boy is in your face, goofy, licky, and like that. Buddha Bear, not so much.

But. If someone — another dog, a cat, or a man with a hat (more on that later) — looks or acts in a way that Big Boy takes as being the least bit of a threat to me or someone in the family, he has a face and a bark that will make anyone who doesn't know him think twice about getting closer or acting smart. Believe me, no one messes with with me when Big Boy's around. And he's around almost all the time. I do go to school by myself, though. But you know if I'm ever the least bit scared or worried when I'm on my own, I just have to channel a little bit of Big Boy and my potential troubles turn tail and quickly walk away. CYA!

I THINK YOU CAN TELL I'M GETTING pretty good at taking care of both my dogs. And I think my dogs think that, too. But, I have to say, the first year was a blur of new experiences. I learned quickly that Big Boy was smart. It didn't take him long to realize we were trying to get him to do certain things at certain times. And though he might not know why we wanted him to do something, mostly he did what we wanted him to. Mostly, but he was a dog, you know. So sometimes . . .

LATER ON, I LEARNED FROM OUR trainer that Big Boy is a protective breed of dog who naturally wants to patrol the boundary of our yard once a night. And when people would pass by on the sidewalk, on the other side of the fence, he would would bark. Not a yip-yip squeaky bark, but a deep-throated, "I'm-going-to-tear-you-in-half" sound that would make the person jump in surprise, and maybe a little fear.

In Africa, the job of the South African mastiff — the kind of dog that Big Boy is — is to keep the lions at bay and away from the herds of goats. Yeah, you heard right. Big Boy is the kind of dog that makes lions jump and run away. Kind of makes you wonder what it was that made him afraid of people and new stuff in general. But, both those things were true.

If a person to whom I was introducing Big Boy felt fear, Big Boy felt it too and made himself bigger. Or least seem to be bigger. So every time we met someone new, it was my job to make sure that both sides of the meeting felt safe, But, even when he was barking, Big Boy's little nub of a tail waved enthusiastically.

Big Boy liked most people — but he was afraid of men who wore hats and gloves. I knew from that fear that something had happened to him, probably from some man who owned him before he became part of our family. At first, at night, when he was dreaming, Big Boy would whimper and cry out. It was months before he felt completely safe. And he was never without his buddy, Buddha Bear. Even though Big Boy was bigger, stronger, and scarier, it was actually Buddha Bear who made him feel safe. He knew that Buddha Bear understood what was going on and Big Boy trusted him to do the right thing. For both of them.

Then, in the middle of me getting to know Big Boy, and him getting to know us, something new happened.

SIX MONTHS INTO BIG BOY LEARNING to be part of all of our family, Grandma Betsi came to live with us.

Grandma Betsi is my mother's mother. It's her name that I have, Betsi Jane. Grandma was a dog lover and my mother and I learned our love of dogs, and all animals, from her. Grandma Betsi lived where my mother grew up, about 100 miles away from our house. And when her health began to fade as she got older, she wound up in a place for seniors that wasn't helping her get better, or even be comfortable. So we did for Grandma Betsi what I did for Big Boy — we rescued her. And brought her to live with us.

WE HAD SEVERAL FAMILY DISCUSSIONS about what we needed to do, how we were going to do it, and when. But one of the biggest things we had to talk about was how we thought our dogs and Grandma Betsi would get along. She wasn't very tall and she was very thin. So we were worried that any little bump from our rambunctious (don't you love that word?) giant dogs might knock her over. With not so good results. But, as it turned out, we didn't have to worry.

RESCUING GRANDMA B, which is what I call her now, was almost like rescuing Big Boy. We had to talk to her and convince her she'd be fine living with us. That it wasn't going to be a problem. And that all she had to do was pack up her stuff and get into the car. And when it was time to get her into our car — because we intentionally left the dogs with our favorite dog sitter, Dad — I played the part of Buddha Bear to her Big Boy and I got in the back seat first and coaxed Grandma B to get in with me.

THE TRIP HOME WAS PRETTY EASY. We stopped at a Baskin-Robbins for ice cream and that helped all of us chill out. Sorry.

WHEN WE GOT HOME, Dad let the dogs out of the house while Grandma B was still in the car. When she opened the door, both of them walked up real slow to her, bowed their heads to be scratched, took the dog treats she had hidden in her purse, backed off a few feet, and gobbled them down as Mom helped Grandma out of the car and into the house.

It didn't take long before Grandma was settled in the armchair she had given mom years ago and our two giant dogs sat along side her chair like book-ends. It was clear who was in charge and who was going to be safe in our house. And, as the queen, Grandma B made sure her favorite dogs got plenty of treats and snuggles. At night, Buddha Bear slept on Grandma B's bed while Big Boy first circled the perimeter of our yard, and then of her bed, and made sure no lions could get past him and harm his queen. In short, starting from first glance, the three of them became buddies.

I guess dogs and grandmas just know things.

Gramma B and Big Boy
Sharing breakfast.
Sort of.

Chapter Four

The Lesson of the Twin Guardians

EVEN GOOD BUDDIES HAVE TO LEARN how to get along. I mean, I have some friends who, how shall I say this? Say nicely, I mean. Okay. A few of my friends, whom I love very much, can be a touch dramatic? Bossy? You know? I'm sure you do.

It was the same with Grandma B and the dogs. Each of them had their own character, the way they would normally talk and behave when there was no one else around. And if each of them allowed their own character full rein, well, you know, there certainly could have been some pretty vocal conflicts.

But from the first, that never happened.

If you took the time to sit and watch them all interacting and behaving — which I certainly did — these are the things you would have noticed.

ONE

GRANDMA B WAS DEFINITELY THE QUEEN B. Sorry about that, but it was true. She was the leader of the pack. What she wanted, she got, and the dogs were, I don't know, Glad? Proud? Honored? To make that happen. Now, I don't mean that Grandma B was demanding or bossy because she was anything but that. You could tell by watching her and how she and the dogs interacted, that she had a lifetime of experience with dogs. She knew what to do, and they did what she guided them to do, and they did it gladly. It was clear they knew they needed her to be in charge.

GRANDMA B ALWAYS MADE SURE she had something to reward her guardians in her pockets. Some treat that they would sit still to receive. Or lie down. And what I noticed was that even when Grandma wasn't passing out treats, the way she looked at her buddies caused them to respond as if she DID have a treat in her hand. I guess that's what training is all about — creating the behavior you want with nothing more than a look. I'm wondering if I can do that with Jimmy. I'm thinking I'm gonna give that one a try, whenever I see him again.

Now that I think about it, I don't believe I've mentioned recently — oops, or maybe at all — where Jimmy is these days. He's a sophomore in college, and he's studying something to do with engineering. I don't really recall exactly what his field of study is this month, but I know he's changed his mind a few times. And may still do so again. But I do know that he's in the first year of his NROTC program and in the summers when he's not in school, he'll be doing camps and retreats and stuff. I know that sounds like fun, but I'm not so sure it isn't really hard work. But it's what Jimmy wants and I know he'll be good at it. When he graduates from school, he'll serve full time in the Marines for at least several years. I miss him now. By the end of all that, I wonder if I'll still know him. Well, I'm pretty sure that no matter how much he changes and learns, he'll still be my big brother, Jimmy. The guy who helped me rescue Big Boy. Hoo-RAH! (That's Marine Talk for "You Go Girl." Can I say that about a guy?)

FROM THE FIRST DAY THAT GRANDMA B was home being watched over by the boys, Mom and I started calling Big Boy and Buddha Bear "The Twin Guardians." Sounds like one of those Marvel movies, doesn't it? And in a strange way, at times it seemed like it was. "Space Granny and her Twin Guardians Conquer the Universe!!!!!" Okay. A touch much, I know. But you get the idea.

TWO

AS MUCH AS BIG BOY AND BUDDHA BEAR shared the honor of being one of The Twin Guardians, each of them had clearly-defined roles that fell, not surprising in the least, along the lines of their individual, natural personalities. Big Boy was The Great Protector, Buddha Bear The Great Watcher.

I've told you about Big Boy being a protector breed of dog, the kind trained in Africa to scare away the lions. Every time I think about that, or tell someone about it, I'm still amazed. My dog, who listens to me, my mom, and Grandma B when we tell him what to do (at least he listens most of the time!) scaring away lions!? I never would have thought I'd have a dog for a pet that lions would be afraid of. But I did.

ANYWAY. SO BIG BOY HAD THE ROLE of the Great Protector. His self-appointed job was to keep all lions (just joking) and scary and mean people away from Grandma B and keep her safe. As you can imagine, he did that very well. Sometimes, though, he could almost be too much. To make sure that Big Boy, in his passion to keep Grandma B safe, didn't inadvertently cause any pain, when visitors came to our house, we would put Big Boy and Buddha Bear into their sleeping pens where they could be noisy but not rambunctious!!! In reality, Buddha Bear would have remained quite calm and under control and wouldn't require being put in his pen. But it worked better for Big Boy if he could see that what was happening to him was something the humans did with all their dogs when guests came. And that being put in your crate was not a punishment of any sort for Big Boy. It's like when parents treat brothers and sisters in the same way. No special deals for favorite sons. Or daughters.

SOMETIMES I THINK I MAKE IT SOUND like living with Big Boy was something to be endured. I don't mean that at all. But at 150 pounds of muscle, Big Boy was certainly an imposing force to be reckoned with. Which is what made him such a good protector. And drove the lions crazy. But because of Big Boy's size and his muscle power, even the slightest movement, especially with speed, could knock someone down. Once he felt a threat to one of us — or at least he felt there *could* be a threat — he would move quickly, and without thinking, directly at the threat in the hope of either driving it away or physically intercepting it before it got close enough to us where it could cause damage.

FOR MUCH OF BIG BOY'S EXPERIENCES IN LIFE, he knew he had the size advantage over real and perceived threats. Unless that treat came in the form of a man with a hat — and then he would only stand his ground and growl, trying to bluff his opponent into backing off. So the sleeping crate was a good beginning to an unknown relationship. And almost always, that relationship turned into one of being friends and Big Boy could be let out of his crate. Not that totally friendly advances by Big Boy couldn't knock someone down, but somehow Big Boy always seemed to know the correct amount of contact that was acceptable.

ONE OF THE GREAT TIMES WE'D HAVE was when me, Grandma B, Big Boy, and Buddha Bear would sit around the fire pit outside and chew the fat. That's camping-speak for talking. Actually, what would happen was that Big Boy and Buddha Bear would listen and eat treats that Grandma B would throw to them every so often, I'd ask questions and listen, and Grandma B would tell stories about growing up with dogs — and about other things. I guess she didn't think the dogs would be interested in her garden-growing stories, so she pretty much stuck with stuff they'd know about. But I always thought with enough treats, our dogs would even listen to Dad talk about mowing the lawn.

And treats? Grandma B knew all about the best ones. Of course there are the ones you can buy and they're good but they do have a lot of salt which might not be the best thing for a dog, especially if they gobbled them down at the rate that Grandma B would toss them out. So Grandma B used peanut butter to make her own treats. Neither dog felt cheated that she hadn't bought the latest treat on the market. Her treats apparently were pretty darn good.

ONE OF THE DISCUSSIONS I REMEMBER most vividly was when Grandma B got to talking about her favorite dog, who, of course, had gone over the Rainbow Bridge many years ago.

"MY DOG'S NAME WAS TUFFINGTON, but everyone called him Tuffy," she said. "He was a Golden Retriever. One day, a pickup truck with a load of puppies in the back pulled up to my antique shop. I fell in love at first sight. Tuffy stayed with us almost 15 years. I loved him. Everyone loved him. One night, when I came home from work, Tuffy was waiting. He jumped into my arms and died of a heart attack."

NEEDLESS TO SAY, WHEN I HEARD that story I went totally silent. What does one say other than, "Oh, Grandma B! I'm so sorry."

"Don't be, Betsi Jane. I know Tuffy waited all day until I got home and once he jumped into my arms, he looked at me and just let go. There wasn't any better way to tell me he loved me than to die in my arms. We buried him the back yard.

"After Tuffy died, I wasn't sure if I'd ever own another dog. I wasn't sure I could ever live with the pain of losing another dog I loved like I loved Tuffington."

"I know what you mean," I said as I looked at Big Boy and Buddha Bear and wondered how I would feel when it was their turn to cross the bridge. That's not something I ever really thought about before, but when Grandma B brought up her story of Tuffington and his last moments, I knew it was something everyone who owns a dog will have to deal with one day. Dogs live so many years fewer than people that it's certain they will pass away before we do. Which means we'll be left here, feeling sad about them being gone. But at the same time, feeling happy over all the great memories they have created with us. Memories that will surely last our lifetimes, just like the memories that Grandma B's dog Tuffington created for her to remember in her later years. Like the memories she was telling now.

I REALLY LOVED GRANDMA B. She had so many great stories to share with us. Stories like this one.

"IN LIFE, YOU HAVE TO LEARN to let go. Grief is part of living and loving. Your dogs never really leave your heart, you know. Their love and daily lessons live with you long after they pass. You have two wonderful dogs, Betsi Jane, who are creating great stories for you. And for me, too. But, they will die. And grief will follow. My advice is to realize that's what life is all about. We should focus on the gift their lives have given us. And not on the pain of loss their passing creates in us. That pain is short. Their love is long. But honestly? Saying goodbye was the hardest thing I have ever done.

"LOSING A DOG, A FRIEND, OR A CHILD — and I've lost all three — is painful. But what I learned is this. You can't let the hurt your heart feels stop you from loving again. What you have to do is hold the love and lessons they shared by being with you in your heart and your memory. Once you realize they never really leave your heart, their love and daily lessons live on. You just have to focus on the gift their lives created and not on the pain of their loss. Once they're gone, you still have to continue to live and love every day."

TALKING ABOUT OUR DOGS DYING was a confusing feeling, something I had never really though about. But I was glad I had the opportunity to understand it from someone who had experienced the loss of a favorite pet and to understand how she dealt with it. When we rescued Grandma B, it never occurred to me that she would actually be helping me like that. I'm not sure what I expected but I know I never thought we would be talking about dogs, death, and dying. And the joy our dog friends produced in our lives. Or the courage that joy and love would create in helping us move on with our lives. Or with passing along that love to another pet.

THAT WAS SOMETHING I KNEW I would be dealing with. Someday. I just didn't know then how soon that day would be.

The Twin Guardians.

Chapter Five

Grandma's Bridge

GROWING UP, I NEVER THOUGHT of our house as being small. We each had our own bedrooms. There was a large kitchen with a table that held all of us. A dining room for when we had company or a party. A living room, and a library where Grandma held forth, her Two Guardians by her side. I never thought the library was especially small and yet it was packed so full, you almost couldn't walk through it. Which never seemed to stop the dogs from dashing full-speed to the front door when they'd spot a squirrel in the yard. And nothing ever seemed to stop them from barking full volume at times like that, either. Unless Grandma was bribing them with a treat. How she knew she could upstage a wild squirrel was something I never thought to ask her. But she always could. Her supply of magic tricks seemed endless.

HOW FULL DO I MEAN? Well, this tiny library held the big crate for Big Boy and a slightly smaller crate for Buddha Bear for when we had visitors. A little couch for those visitors to sit on, Betsi's chair and side table, a chair for the music therapist to sit at her keyboard, a chair for the art therapist and a table for her supplies. I was impressed with the art that Grandma B turned out. It may not have been museum quality, but it was really good. At least I thought so, and isn't that what art appreciation is all about? My dad always said, "I may not know much about art but I know what I like." I think he may have heard that somewhere.

Obviously, Mom thought Grandma was a pretty good artist, too. She framed all of Grandma B's pictures and has been giving out some of them as gifts at Christmas and birthdays. Grandma B called the painting she made of our house with the big tree out front, "My safe place." Mom gave it to me for graduation and I have it hanging in my room at school. And yes, I bring it home for the summer!

WHEN THE MUSIC THERAPIST CAME, Grandma B would pull out songs from her memory and sing them to us while she painted. I learned a bunch of them and sang along while Big Boy would hum to the music and Buddha Bear closed his eyes. It was always a magical moment.

One time — and I'm not sure this was exactly magical, but it certainly was remarkable — in the middle of all the music and fun, Grandma B told us the very hard story of the death of her son, Jimmy, at the age of five. She told us what happened, how she felt, and how she had continued to feel all the rest of her life. Then she began to paint a big circle using several shades of lavender (still my favorite color). We watched, not saying a word. When her circle was completed, she said to us, "This is my pain."

On that day when she told this story, with the music and painting going on, you could actually see that she was letting go of her pain — for the first time in her life — at the age of 85. Mom told me later that Grandma B had held on to that grief for her entire life and it weighed her down. It was a very special moment for her, and for all of us in the room.

FOR ME, I WOULDN'T UNDERSTAND what all this meant until months later. Until then, I didn't know what to do with grief or how to support someone who was grieving. It was then that I learned that there are no words to fill the hole in your heart — but words and cards, story telling and sharing, and just sitting quietly together make grief less heavy.

When Grandma took her nap that day, I sat down next to Mom. I could tell she had been crying. Honestly, I felt I might have been doing a little of that myself. But anyway, I asked her about what Grandma B had just told us.

"ALL MY LIFE, I'VE LEARNED A LOT from my mother," my mother said. "She taught me how to cook, garden, speak, and write. She explained what was good etiquette and why it was important, and the joy of filling our home with friends and family. She taught me that our pets are our family, too.

"And she would talk about grief. She said that holding the pain of grief inside you all your life is a burden, especially when it comes from losing someone you love. But until today, I never really knew that she was still carrying it around for my brother and her dogs. But when I saw it disappear from her, like it was floating out of her chest in a cloud. I couldn't believe it. But I watched it disappear through the ceiling of the library — I wanted to cry. But I didn't. Instead, I thought about what she had been hauling around inside of her all those years, and how the music and good memories and painting and all of us being there with her actually lifted the grief right off her heart and made her smile. To be honest, it made me smile, too."

I SAT THERE FOR AWHILE, THINKING about what Mom had just said and what I had seen. Then, I leaned over to her, put my arms around her, and said. "I love you, Mom. And Grandma B, too."

And I smiled as I looked at the ceiling.

. . .

IT WAS IN THE SECOND MONTH of my Junior year in High School that Grandma B fell and broke her pelvis. The day it happened, I was in school. It was a Thursday. When I got home to walk the dogs, Mom told me that Grandma B had been out in the garden and that Buddha Bear came dashing in to the kitchen, insisting that Mom come outside with her. How, you ask, does a dog "insist?" Well in Buddha Bear's language it meant that he pushed his head against my mom's leg and moved her toward the door he'd just come in through. And he didn't stop until Mom was outside.

Mom said that once Buddha Bear had pushed her out to the garden, Grandma B was lying on the path and saying, "Leslie, I think I've broken something. It really hurts."

And where was Big Boy all this time? He was standing next to Grandma B, keeping all the lions away, of course.

NOW WHEN A PERSON BREAKS their pelvis, there is almost no need to ever have a cast. The muscles around the pelvis seem to hold the bones in place. So, with a little rest, a broken pelvis heals pretty much by itself. That doesn't mean it doesn't hurt. Grandma B said it did and I took her word for that. But you do need a lot of rest; and for awhile you can't or shouldn't walk. A person with a broken pelvis might need crutches, a walker, or a wheel chair. Grandma B had all three.

I have to tell you that Grandma B was a really tough "old bird," as she liked to say about herself. And she got around first with her wheel chair and then her walker. While she did have crutches, like I said, she thought they were too hard on her arms, so they sat in the corner the whole time she was recovering.

AT FIRST, WE HIRED SOME CAREGIVERS to come in and help us help her — I was in school and so was Anne. Jimmy was in his first year of college, so he wasn't around at all for Grandma's adventure, as she called it. And Mom and Dad still had their duties and their jobs — so we needed the help.

ONE OF THE INTERESTING THINGS that happened was that when the caregivers would move Grandma B, that slight movement would hurt and she would moan lightly. But even though it wasn't much of a moan, it was enough to put both dogs on high alert and they would low-growl to warn the nurses they were paying attention and not to hurt their queen. It didn't take long until Grandma B suggested to Mom that we didn't need the caregivers, just in case the dogs got too overprotective and tried to push them away, which they MIGHT have done if they thought Grandma B was actually being hurt. Fortunately, Mom agreed, let the caregivers go to help someone who wasn't blessed with Two Guardians, and then she talked Grandma B into going into a rehab center.

Which, in and of itself, was good and bad.

The good was that Grandma B had constant attention paid to her and she was getting daily supervised walking, first on a treadmill, than later around the hallways with a nurse always at her elbow, just in case. And no, not because there was any fear of lions.

The bad, was that in spite of the tremendous care she was getting, Grandma B hated being there. She wanted to come home so badly that she . . . well, just listen.

AT CHRISTMAS, GRANDMA B WALKED by herself with no help and no walker. All that rehabilitation had gotten her fixed up so that for the first time since she had fallen, she was on her own. Now, you might think that was something to cheer about. And while it might have been for most folks, for Grandma B it was the push she needed to get what she wanted. And what she wanted more than anything, was to come home to us, to her over-crowded-with-stuff library, and her Two Guardians.

SO THE SECOND DAY SHE COULD WALK, she got out of bed, got dressed in street clothes, and walked down the hall to the lobby, where she laid down on her back in the center of the room and spread her arms wide and said as loudly as she could, "I'm not moving from here until someone comes to get me and takes me home."

NOW, LET ME TELL YOU, WHEN Grandma B got something in her mind, it would be a waste of your time to try and talk her out of it. So, since it was a Saturday, Mom and I piled in the car, drove down to the rehab center, picked her up, and brought her home, where we had Christmas dinner, exchanged presents, and watched Grandma B fall asleep in her chair, safe because her Two Guardians were at her side.

ON NEW YEAR'S DAY, we had sauerkraut, pork loin, and mashed potatoes. Jimmy was still home and Grandma B was in pretty good spirits; it was a wonderful day. Unfortunately, there weren't going to be many more days like that.

In May, she fell and broke her hip. Unlike her broken pelvis, her broken hip needed to be operated on and placed in a cast and that was going to put Grandma B flat on her back in bed. But since we'd moved a hospital bed into her bedroom, we knew she would be comfortable. Mom said she'd take time off work, Jimmy was already back in school but due to get out in a few weeks, and so were Anne and I. Grandma B, however, began to, well, there's only one way to say this. Grandma B began to fade.

She had decided she didn't want to have any surgery, even though she was in pain. (You remember what I told you about when Grandma B made up her mind.) The doctor prescribed some pain relievers which would help. But we all knew, even Grandma B, that she was slipping away from us. Her time was coming to an end.

And kind of like Tuffy, two days later, when Mom came home from shopping, Grandma B smiled at my mother, said thanks to all of us, closed her eyes and said, "I can see the bridge from here."

And she was gone.

The next day was Mother's Day and we all sat around and told Grandma B stories. And laughed. And smiled.

And we cried.

And we sang her favorite song, "Somewhere, Over the Rainbow."

BUT MOST OF ALL WE WERE GLAD. Glad for all the time we had to share with that wonderful woman, my Grandma B.

Gramma B and her Art Instuctor.

Big Boy loved to leap.

Chapter Six

It Isn't Easy Saying Goodbye

IT WAS ONE WEEK BEFORE CHRISTMAS of my senior year — seven months after Grandma B died — when Big Boy jumped off Grandma's empty bed onto the floor and screamed in pain.

If you've ever heard a dog of any size, much less a 150-pound Guardian, scream in pain, you know what pain sounds like. Their pain hurts your ears. A lot.

I ran to him and he looked up at me with eyes that said he had no idea what had just happened but that he knew he didn't want it to happen again. Fortunately, Jimmy was home from school and, between us, we calmed Big Boy down and pulled the bedding from his cage over to where he was lying and gently lifted him on top of it.

Mom, being the good mom she is, came swiftly — but calmly — into the library, with her phone in her hand, making an emergency appointment with the vet.

YOU MAY WONDER HOW WE COULD move Big Boy gently. Well, Jimmy's really strong, and so am I. But the real reason, as we found out later, was that Big Boy had lost 30 pounds since Grandma passed. We knew he was looking almost like he did when we first brought him home, a lot of skin and bones. But we had thought it was because he was grieving and not eating. Well, not as much, at least.

And while there was no doubt that was partly true, we only found out the real reason later that afternoon. At the vet's.

The answer was the Big C, cancer.

BIG BOY HAD CANCER OF THE BONE that had spread. "Most likely, the cancer started where his leg was broken years ago," the vet said. "And, I'm sorry to say, with the rate at which it's spread, Big Boy doesn't have much time left. The logical thing to do is to amputate his leg. That should give him at least another year, maybe a few months more. Or less."

All three of us were stunned. Big Boy hobbling around on three legs? It was hard to imagine our wild, hard-running dog reduced to a three-legged crawl. But that's what his future looked like. At least to the vet.

"Why don't you take Big Boy home with you and talk it over and let me know what you'd like to do?" he asked.

We couldn't think of anything else to do, so that's what we did.

"I CAN'T BELIEVE THIS," I SAID, my eyes filled with tears. "I don't want to lose Big Boy. He's a part of the family. It's not fair. What did he ever do to deserve cancer?"

"I know," said Jimmy, who's not much of talker when it comes to sharing his feelings. Unless it's about our Cleveland Browns or the Marines. But we were talking about Big Boy and how we felt. So, for Jimmy, that was a long speech. But then, he surprised me.

"I wasn't sure when you brought Big Boy home. I knew that dogs don't live as long as people and I was worried you'd get so connected to him and then, poof, he'd be gone. And you'd be crushed. And I was right. When I get my own place, I'll never have a dog. I couldn't stand to go through all this again."

"JIMMY MCLENDON!"

Mom only uses our last names when she's highly upset. So I knew I should pay attention to what she was going to say. Jimmy, it seems, wasn't aware of Mom's code. I knew that because he had started to get up from the couch and wander off somewhere.

"You sit down and listen to me!" Jimmy may not be smart, but he's certainly not dumb, so he sat back down. I mean, he got straight As and all that, but that doesn't necessarily mean you're smart. Or at least it didn't seem to make boys smart. Right?

"I know you've spent almost four years away at school," Mom said, "but I'm certain when you have a chance to really think about you and us and Big Boy, you'll discover you've learned a lot from Big Boy. And Buddha Bear. And you'll see how much they've meant to you. And how much you mean to them. You may not realize this, yet, but when someone has a dog, the dog is part of their life. When a dog has you, you are ALL of their life. It's not an equal arrangement. But that's how it is. And it affects you and will affect you for the rest of your life. And as strange as it might seem right now — when we're in the middle of this hugely emotional situation — that relationship between dogs dying and people living doesn't harden your heart, it softens your heart to be open for the next dog to come along."

"But that's just it, Mom," Jimmy said. "I'm not going to be looking to find another dog."

"Oh, you won't have to look, Jimmy. When the time is right, and you're in the middle of something else entirely, another dog will find you. And your experience with helping your sister rescue Big Boy, and living with him, and teaching him, and learning from him, will make that the most obvious and most right thing to do. And that will happen. Trust me. Another dog will find you. And you know what? You'll be ready to be found."

AT THAT POINT, BOTH BUDDHA BEAR and Big Boy looked at Jimmy with — what was clear to me at least —   love in their eyes. Then Buddha Bear walked over to Jimmy and nudged his hand with his muzzle, the signal that he wanted to be petted.

So, Jimmy petted him.

And Mom laughed — with tears in her eyes. Then Jimmy got up and walked over to Big Boy, who was lying on his blankets with all his toys surrounding him, and Jimmy gave Big Boy a long scratch behind both his ears. "Love you, guys," Jimmy said, his voice sounding choked up, walked to his room, and quietly shut his door.

. . .

FOR THE NEXT SEVERAL HOURS, we all talked about what to do, hugged both dogs, got choked up, and waited for Mom's friend Jennifer to come over and give us some advice.

Jennifer was the one who helped us train Big Boy when we first got him. She has a lot of experience with dogs, both her own and those she's helped train over the years. Jennifer was the one who told us that if Buddha Bear was going to feel weird about Big Boy moving in, he would have let us know how he felt in no uncertain terms. Which is what he did. He told us that he and Big Boy where going to be great friends. And they were. So, we were anxious to hear what Jennifer had to say about Big Boy and his cancer.

But I guess as much as we wanted to hear that, we were really totally unprepared for what she actually had to say.

"I'm sorry to hear about Big Boy's cancer. And I know you all are, too. And now you're faced with a decision about what to do, right?"

None of us could talk, but we could nod our heads yes, so that's what we did.

"There are three choices you can make. The question is which is the best one. I can't tell you what to do, that's your decision. But I can tell you about your choices and how to think about them. Does that work for all of you?"

Again, we nodded silently.

"Like I said, there are three choices. Let's take a look at the good and bad sides of all three. Your first choice is to do nothing. Let the cancer take its course. The good part of that choice for you is that you don't have to analyze things and then make a choice about which action to take. You just let life make the decision for you, and then you live with the consequences. The bad part is that the pain for Big Boy will get worse and worse. Either he will have to endure constantly increasing pain or he will have to be increasingly medicated to mask the pain. Which means he will spend the last days of his life being barely conscious and getting worse and worse. Until he dies."

I couldn't keep silent any longer. "That's not a choice I'd like to take. If it were me in that situation, and I was in pain and dying of cancer, I wouldn't want to spend my last days barely aware of the life I loved so much going unnoticed all around me. Mom? Jimmy? Anne? Your thoughts?"

Jimmy and Anne said nothing but both shook their heads "no." That wasn't the choice for them, either.

"I know this is about Big Boy," Mom said, "but as I've been listening to you, Jennifer, I've been thinking about one of the last conversations I had with my mother before she died. She made me promise not take any extraordinary efforts to save her. And she said she didn't want to be drugged to cover the pain if it made her unaware of the people around her. And I think I'm feeling the same thing for Big Boy. Just letting things happen and trying to mask the pain with medication is no way for an active dog to spend the last days of his life."

"Your mother was right, Leslie," Jennifer said quietly. "But it is a choice that has to be considered. For me personally, I'm on the side of Grandma B."

Me, Jimmy, and Anne smiled and nodded that we agreed. "That's another one for Grandma B," Anne said.

I was impressed. Anne actually spoke up. Way to go, girl.

"OPTION TWO, AND THIS IS THE ONE that the vet prefers, is to amputate the bad leg. The good side? The source of the pain and the cancer is gone forever. The bad? There's likely significant amounts of cancer left in Big Boy's body, which will have to treated with chemo and radiation. And you all know what that can do to the body. Plus, there's no guarantee that treatment will wipe out the cancer. And then, there's the three-legged thing."

"I'm certain Big Boy could learn to walk and even run on three legs," Jimmy said. "He's proved over and over that he's smart and he's tough. But I don't know that he should end his life having to live like that, not being able to chase Buddha Bear and run through the waters of Lake Erie. I'll be hard pressed to vote for this option. What's number three?"

Jennifer looked down at Big Boy, then up at all of us. "This is perhaps the most difficult one — put him to sleep."

Jennifer took a deep breath, and looked at each of us, one at a time. "The good part, if there is any good part to taking the life of your best friend, is that it's quick, gentle, and painless. Big Boy will simply close his eyes, go to sleep, and that will be the end of his pain. The bad part is that, well, Big Boy will walk across the Rainbow Bridge. But he will make that final journey with dignity and not in pain. I know I said I wasn't going to tell you what to do. But I will tell you this — I have personally made this choice several times over the years and I don't regret it.

"SO, THERE THEY ARE, YOUR choices. Any questions?"

FOR SEVERAL MINUTES, we all sat there, not looking at each other, but looking at Big Boy looking at us with his big, sad eyes. Eyes that seemed to know that how his life was going to end was entirely in our hands.

Finally, Mom said, "Betsi Jane. Big Boy is your dog. You saved him from a lonely life and a certain early death. You brought him into our world, into our family. You were responsible for him having five great years with us. I think it's only right that you should be the one who decides, under the conditions he faces, the best way for him to get across that bridge. What do you think?"

I was crying so hard, I had a hard time thinking, much less talking. Buddha Bear got up and walked over to me and nuzzled my leg. I think he was telling me something. So I took a deep breath and said, "Mom. This is too hard! All I can think if of is — what would Grandma B have done?"

"She told you," Jimmy said. "She would have let Big Boy go with dignity, with her arms around him. Just like Tuffy. I think that's what we should do. What do you, think, Beej? Can you follow in Grandma B's path and lead Big Boy on the path to the Rainbow Bridge?"

DO YOU THINK THERE WAS EVEN a choice, there? I got up and walked slowly over to Big Boy, put my arms around him and said, "You know that no matter what happens I will love you forever. We all will. But I don't want to see you trying to tough it out and live in pain, or trying bravely to walk on three legs for the rest of your life. I just want you to know that you are my forever dog and I will never forget you."

Never.

*Big Boy ready
to cross the bridge.*

Chapter Seven

Time for Another Ending

IT'S ALMOST A YEAR SINCE THE PASSING of Grandma B and Big Boy. In that time, I started a daily diary. That way, ideas, thoughts, sayings, and the things I've learned are available for me to read when I need to be inspired and provide a boost to get through the day. This morning — it's about two weeks before I go home for the summer — I have been reading through my diary to psych myself up with powerful and good thoughts before walking into our living room at home and realizing how much I miss Big Boy.

ONE OF THE INTERESTING THINGS that happened this year was that Mom decided to write me letters every week or so. She said it was easier for her to gather her thoughts if she wrote them down, rather than call, or heaven forbid, text. At least, that's what she said. Surprisingly, I found myself doing things the old way — I started writing her back. I guess I figured if writing was good for her understanding, then reading the written word (MY letters!) would be good, too.

Anyway.

HERE ARE A FEW PARTS FROM some of our letters over the last year. I hope you like them as much as I do.

Dear Betsi Jane

I am a letter writer. That's how I communicate, how I keep my thoughts in logical order. So, forgive the letter. BTW, I am aware it's not a text. IKR. (I hope that's the right abbreviation!) But it IS typed!

Anyway, I've been thinking a lot about Big Boy and Grandma B — no surprise there. And about the pain and grief we experience when someone we love dies. And, then about how to make yourself go on, and not quit.

I don't think you can get over grief. That's just my opinion. It's not a cold or the flu. It's not something you catch and then wait until you get better. You need to come to an understanding of your grief as an ache that you need to embrace. You let it wash over you, you look at it, and then it begins to fade away on its own. Not so that it's ever actually gone — but rather that it's part of your life from then on. It's there, it just doesn't hurt as much.

BTW, I don't think that the grief of losing Grandma B is really any different from the grief of losing Big Boy. This may sound obvious, but we will never get another mother or grandmother. But we can choose to get another dog. Therefore, the grief and what happens from living through the grief produce different results. But that doesn't make the grief hurt any differently.

Here are a few bon mots. Those are things that are really good — good like chocolate drops are really good — that I am learning about grief. Tell me what you think.

- Grief is different each time you experience it. It's not exactly the same because each time it's attached to a different loss.

- You can't avoid grief, you have to embrace it as the only way to appreciate what you had.

- Grief can make your chest feel empty. So empty you don't think you can ever again feel love for anyone or anything else again. Soon, though, you discover there is a spring of love in the center of your being that bubbles up and fills your heart space; and slowly, you find fullness again. Your capacity for loving and feeling and receiving returns.

- Learn to love again. Don't be afraid knowing that what you love will die sometime.

- Keep your heart soft and open. If your grief is connected to the passing of your dog, another dog will find you and you need to be ready.

- You will never be without grief. Grief is the reflection of love.

Forgive me if all that sounds too, I don't know, heavy? It's just what I've been thinking about.
Love,

Mom

Dear Mom,

I know exactly what you were talking about in your letter. Even though Buddha Bear was my first dog, our dog leader, I find that I've been thinking a lot about Big Boy, remembering all the good and fun things that happened because of him.

Like how he slept on the bed with someone. When he slept in my bed, he always leaned into me. Like he wanted to be a part of my body. Or at least a part of my skin. But what was interesting was that once Grandma B came to live with us, Big Boy and Buddha bear changed roles. Big Boy slept at the foot of her bed to keep bad things away, and Buddha Bear seemed to realize that Grandma B needed him to be near and so he slept with her. I had no problem with that. I understood it was part of being a dog who felt responsible for an older person. Buddha instinctively knew that Grandma B and I were different. So instead of leaning into her like Big Boy did to me – and maybe causing her pain, or at least to be uncomfortable – he put some space between him and Grandma B when he climbed into bed for the night.

But what I really will never forget is how Grandma B, just before she closed her eyes to fall asleep, would reach out her hand and lay it on Buddha Bear's head and say, "Good-night my old man."

With both of us, Buddha Bear made sure we were safe through the night. In the morning, he licked us and got kissed as his payment for a job well done.

Honestly, I have dozens of stories like this. Maybe next time I'll tell you another one, if you'd like.

But now, I've got to go study. We have final exams next week and I want to do well so they will let me come home to you guys and Buddha Bear.

That was just a joke!

Oh, not about doing well but about them letting me come home!

I'll see you all very soon.

Can't wait!

Betsi Jane,
Your loving daughter!

Dear Betsi Jane,

You ARE my loving daughter. Thank you. And thanks for your letter and the story about the two dogs and my mother. But since I last wrote, I've been thinking a lot, non-stop it seems, about what I said and I've come to realize that I just don't want to get another dog. I really like living with them. And they do make life better, it's true. But it's too painful when they have to cross over that bridge. The grief that passage causes is so overwhelming. I just don't think I can go through all that again.

I think it will be much easier for everyone if we just let the memory of Big Boy be enough. We do have Buddha Bear, after all.

See you when you we come to rescue you and bring you home!

Mom

MOM!!!

I can't believe you actually believe what you're saying!

Yes, we still have Buddha Bear. And yes sometime, perhaps soon, given how old he already is, Buddha Bear will make HIS way over the Rainbow Bridge.

And once that happens, do you plan to be dog-less for the rest of your life? With no fun, no play, no adoration? Just nothing? I don't think you can do that. You're far too giving a person, something you learned from Grandma B – and her Jimmy – I think.

This is how I think about dogs in our life.

Each dog you have is a very important part of your life. They smooth out the corners and fill in the cracks. It's true that they cause an amount of wear and tear, but you know they absolutely love you. Why would you CHOOSE to not let that love into your life?

The difference for the dog is that when you have them, you are their WHOLE life. Everything revolves around you and what you can do for them. And how you treat them. And how you teach them to love. If you disappear, the meaning of their life disappears, too.

When you have a dog, you learn how to love without limits, restrictions, or exceptions. Having a dog changes your life and the dog's life because you love them back with your whole heart. And that, in addition to the specific memories you have of events you shared, is what you bring to a new dog.

For them, you are their much-wiser center-of-life. Your experience with your previous dog gets shared with the new dog. Your old dog has passed over the Rainbow Bridge and is unable to share like Buddha Bear was able to share and teach Big Boy what it meant to be a dog, what it meant to be loved and to love back. Without Buddha Bear, Big Boy might never have reached his full potential. When you are the only center of a new dog's life, it is your responsibility to share what your previous dog taught you. You are the extension of their life, their learning, and their knowledge. And you will become the cosmic extension of your previous pet.

That new relationship will build on the relationship you had with your old dog. It won't replace it – it adds to it, makes it more and better. That's why getting a new dog is important – you get to pass along everything you learned from your first dog to your next one.

Your new dog will benefit from everything you bring to it. But the real surprise is that you will, too. And it won't be at the loss of ANY of the love you shared with your first dog. It will be a glorious new extension of it.

Best of all, you will now have TWO dogs who will have changed YOUR life for the better. Two someones who will have loved you, learned from you, and shared you. And you will be the center of both of their lives.

No matter which side of the Rainbow Bridge they happen to be on.

I hope that you don't think I am being mean or negative about your feelings. I just wanted you to hear what your daughter thinks about the whole thing.

And believe me when I say, I also have considered NOT having another dog. After all, I still have Buddha Bear!

Love,
Betsi Jane

Dear Betsi Jane,

As we discussed on the phone, we'll be there to pick you up next Thursday. Assuming they will let you come home with us and not make you pass another test!

And so I want to warn you about something. It has to do with Buddha Bear.

This week, in the middle of the night, Buddha Bear had what appeared to be a stroke or maybe a seizure. He howled and hobbled around a lot, but he did let me hold him and tell him how much we loved him. It was not very pleasant. Honestly, it was awful.

The next morning, we took him to the vet, who looked him over and said there is nothing that can be done to stop his seizures. It isn't possible, he said, to predict when the next one, if there is a next one, might come or how painful it might be. He said if they got really bad, he could give him painkillers and sedation but I said I would have to talk to you first.

Don't worry, this isn't that talk. We'll do that when you come home.

Also, we have an appointment with a friend of ours who has a puppy he said we could have.

We'll get to meet him together and decide what we want to do. Together.

I hope that's okay with you.

Love,
Mom

PS. A few more thoughts:

• Painful memories will pass, but the years of joy will remain. Keep your heart soft so you can find the love of another animal.

• Grief steals your energy and takes up space in your mind. Grief is like a pool of water that reflects the depth of the love you have given and have received.

• Painful memories immediately recede – if slowly – while the lessons of love you experience with those who have just left you begin to take center stage in your life.

• Don't try to close grief down – to deny that it's there in your heart. Let time and the support of others carry you gently on the wings of the one you loved and have lost.

Chapter Eight

Jumping on the Bridge

WHEN MOM CAME TO THE DOOR of my dorm room, I was just putting the last of my clothes into my suitcase. Everything else was packed in boxes I'd gotten from the grocery store that all the students use. Well, not ALL of them. But me and friends did.

Anyway.

"SO WHAT'S THE STORY WITH BUDDHA BEAR?" I asked.

"We'll have plenty of time for that once we get the car packed and head out. Okay?"

"I guess." And so, we hauled everything out to Mom's car — Dad was with Anne at her soccer game — grabbed some fries and a couple of Cokes at Sonic, and headed back home. Mom driving and talking, and me listening intently.

"Okay," Mom said. "Over the last several weeks . . ."

"Several WEEKS? This has been going on for WEEKS? I didn't know about this!!"

"Keep calm, Betsy Jane. It's a long trip. But, yes, weeks. At first, none of us were sure what was going on with Buddha Bear. During the first event, I guess you could say, we thought he'd just had a bad dream. And that maybe it was triggered by something he'd caught outside and eaten."

"Oooh! That's yucky. Odious, even."

"Odious?"

"Yeah, that's a cool word that means disgusting."

"Oh, thanks for the insight."

"Well, it was something I learned this year and this was my first chance to use it in public and impress someone."

"Well, it worked. I'm impressed. But meanwhile, back to our conversation. It was a couple of weeks later when Buddha Bear had his next event, this one apparently was much stronger because it made him cry out a lot more and dash around, rubbing his head on the carpet.

"The one after that was right before I wrote to tell you about them and it was really pretty bad. The worst."

"That's really worrisome. What can we do? I don't want to lose Buddha Bear, too. Big Boy and Grandma B were enough. Please!"

"Well, why don't you close your eyes and get some rest while I drive. Unless you want to drive and I'll nap."

SO, I DROVE HOME AND MOM TOOK THE NAP. She snored lightly while I had heavy thoughts about Buddha Bear and his Rainbow Bridge.

. . .

"STROKES AND SEIZURES ARE NOT the same thing," the vet said. "A stroke is when the flow of blood in the brain is disrupted. When a dog has a stroke, his legs often stiffen up, he goes unconscious, and he starts to shake. This can last up to two minutes.

"A seizure happens when there is a burst of electricity in the brain. The symptoms are more progressive as the seizure occurs, often starting with being unsteady, having glazed eyes, then foaming at the mouth, followed by losing consciousness and control of bodily functions. This can last as much as five minutes. Which sounds like what's happening to Buddha Bear, doesn't it, Betsi Jane?"

"Well, honestly, I wasn't there when they happened but from what Mom said, it sounds like a seizure. Right Mom?"

"That's what I think. What do we do now, doctor?"

"Unfortunately, I think Buddha Bear's seizures are more likely caused by his age and his heredity than by something that can be treated with preventative medicine. But to be sure, I'll do a blood and urine test to see if there's anything there that might give us a better clue. In the meantime, make sure his water is always available and feed him when he's hungry, not just not at a specific time of day. And

hug and love him. And especially when he's con-
vulsing, you should hug him securely.

"Good luck, Buddha Bear. And I want you two to keep
in touch with us and update us about his situation. Okay?

"Okay, doc," I said. "I'll be on it, you can be sure."

. . .

"HEY, MOM," I SAID AFTER WE HAD gotten home and
made Buddha Bear comfortable in his bed, "I just
noticed that Buddha Bear's tail has been cropped.
What happened?"

"Well, after Big Boy died and you went off to
school, it looked like Buddha Bear was trying to make
himself be happy again and he started wagging his
tail really hard and all the time. It's what the vet said
they call 'Happy Tail.' When he wagged it hard and
hit a hard surface, the end of the tail got damaged.
And that caused him to lick it constantly, which
stopped it from getting fully healed. So every time
he hit his tail, it got worse. The vet told us to try a
sock with an ACE bandage on it but that didn't work
at all. There was blood sprayed all over the house and
Buddha Bear was going crazy over his tail.

"So we took him to the vet and he docked it.
Once that happened, Buddha Bear was fine."

"Why didn't you tell me this sooner? Why am I
only hearing this now?"

"Your dad and I, along with the vet, decided it
wasn't necessary to tell you about it right after Big
Boy died. A dog having his tail docked is a very com-
mon procedure. And the vet said once it was done,

Buddha Bear would be alright and no one would notice his tail was a lot shorter."

"Okay, I guess. Is there anything else you haven't told me?"

"No, I don't think so. Just that Anne got straight As on her report cards every grading period this year. We were all proud of her accomplishment."

"That's swell. But what did you tell me about a new dog?"

"Ah, well, ah . . ."

. . .

"HE'S SO CUTE MOM, BUT HE'S nowhere near as big as either Big Boy or Buddha Bear. Will he grow?"

"He's a French Bulldog," Mom said. "Miguel said we should try another, smaller breed of dog so we didn't get into a continuous cycle of comparing him to Big Boy. Or even to Buddha Bear. So, no, he won't grow in size. Just in love. And because of his crooked tail, Miguel named him Crook."

FOR THE NEXT SEVERAL WEEKS, I played with Crook, showed him the sacred pee spot, taught him to sit and shake, and all the things you train a dog to do and understand. As I did all this, I realized I was calling on what I had learned from living with and training both Buddha Bear and Big Boy. And I began to understand what someone had said about using what you learned from your old dogs to help your new dog get ahead more quickly. I have to say, I was really having fun.

Then, one night, Buddha Bear started moaning and staggering around. I got up from watching TV and put my arms around him and told him things would be alright. When Mom came in, we had been at that for more than five minutes. Five minutes being the decision time in a seizure to determine if you should call the vet or not. It was time to make that call.

. . .

THE NEXT DAY, WE WERE SITTING in the vet's office. Well, Mom and the doc were sitting in chairs, but I was sitting on the floor with my arms around Buddha Bear, who looked confused and like he might be in pain.

"Well folks, we're at decision time again. And as we've talked about before, you know there's really not any medicine that will cure Buddha Bear's seizures and at his age, well, realistically he's only going get worse and be in more and worse pain. And that will be as hard on you two as the seizures are on him. Your thoughts?"

"Betsi Jane, Buddha Bear is your dog. What should we do?" Mom asked.

"Well as difficult as it was with Big Boy, I think the only realistic option is to admit we have come to the end of the path. And in front of us is the first step onto the Rainbow Bridge. Doc, can I hold him while you give the shot or do we have to strap him to the table?"

"Of course, you should hold him. I wouldn't have it any other way."

AND SO I DID I EXACTLY WHAT I wanted to do, the vet did what he had to do, and Buddha Bear did what he always did — he looked at me and licked my face. Then he closed his eyes, and — I really believe this — he actually jumped up on the Rainbow Bridge and made a mad dash for Big Boy. And, I also believe that waiting on the other side of that bridge was Grandma B with Tuffy in her arms and her son Jimmy by her side.

That's what I think happened.

And no one can change my mind.

The three Bs, over the bridge.

Epilogue

The End of the Second Beginning

IT'S NOW A MONTH LATER, AND I'M going through things in my head one more time, trying to crystallize everything I've learned in the last several years about love, living, and dying. And floating around in there are all those thoughts and sayings about how love and grief are necessary and interconnected, and how they help each of us get through the difficult times of life much better. And how no one really wants to talk much about how they feel about people and dogs dying.

And while all of that is very true and very valuable — and I keep it all in my mind — in my opinion, so should you. Let me share what I think all of that boils down to. And how this is really the best way to live the rest of your life. Here goes. I hope you like this.

Oh, and one more thing. Between me and Mom, we now have three new dogs: Minster, Winston, and Crook. And I think I heard Mom mention on the phone the other day that she was interested in adopting a pair of French Bulldogs.

How's that for someone who once said, very firmly, that she would never again go through the grief of losing a dog she loved?

But we've all changed because of our experiences with Grandma B, Big Boy, and Buddha Bear and their departures over Rainbow Bridge.

I know I have.

Though I was once unsure if I would ever have another dog, living with Mom and her troupe of FIVE — yes I said FIVE! — dogs made me think and realize this.

Whenever there was a dog around, my life was always better — because I had someone to love and someone to love me. And even though that's absolutely true, at least for me, I have thought this all through and decided that before I get another dog — or two — I will wait until I'm out of college, have a job, and my own place.

And then I will either find a dog or be ready when a dog finds me. And when he or she does find me, I will have a stockpile of experiences ready to share that will make both our lives infinitely better. That dog will never replace either Big Boy or Buddha Bear. It will just expand the love I have in my heart.

TMP!   [That's my plan!]

The Rainbow Bridge
— Author Unknown

JUST THIS SIDE OF HEAVEN IS A PLACE called Rainbow Bridge. When an animal dies that has been especially close to someone here, that pet goes to Rainbow Bridge. There are meadows and hills for all of our special friends so they can run and play together. There is plenty of food, water, and sunshine, and our friends are warm and comfortable.

All the animals who had been ill and old are restored to health and vigor. Those who were hurt or maimed are made whole and strong again, just as we remember them in our dreams of days and times gone by. The animals are happy and content, except for one small thing; they each miss someone very special to them, who had to be left behind.

They all run and play together, but the day comes when one suddenly stops and looks into the distance. His bright eyes are intent. His eager body quivers. Suddenly he begins to run from the group, flying over the green grass, his legs carrying him faster and faster.

You have been spotted, and when you and your special friend finally meet, you cling together in joyous reunion, never to be parted again. The happy kisses rain upon your face; your hands again caress the beloved head, and you look once more into the trusting eyes of your pet, so long gone from your life but never absent from your heart.

Then you cross Rainbow Bridge . . . Together.

The Boys on the Beach.

About the Authors

LESLIE YERKES IS AN AUTHOR, and motivational speaker. She is an organizational development/ change management consultant in Cleveland, Ohio. She founded Catalyst Consulting Group, Inc. in 1987 with a simple philosophy: People are basically good, well-intentioned, courageous, and able to learn. Her job is to provide a framework in which people can draw on their own inner resources to find creative solutions.

A cum laude graduate of Wittenberg University, Leslie earned her Master of Science in Organizational Development from Case Western Reserve University. She has taught at John Carroll University, Baldwin Wallace College, The Mandel School of Applied Social Science, and is on the faculty at the Weatherhead Dively Center for Executive Education.

Her business goal is to help people create sustainable organizations. Her life goal is to create the framework in which people can draw on their own resources to find creative solutions. A measure of Leslie's success as a business leader and consultant is that she first applies to herself the principles in which she engages her clients. Her clients have included Chrysler Corporation, The Cleveland Clinic Foundation, Lake Hospital System, The United Church of America, Westfield Companies, and Mittal Steel USA. A sub specialty of Leslie's is making non-profits healthy and sustainable.

Leslie is the author of six previous books that have been translated into more than a dozen languages and have sold hundreds of thousands of copies worldwide.

Big Boy and Buddha Bear are featured on the website lostfoundandforever.com.

Leslie's website is www.leslieyerkes.com.

RANDY MARTIN BEGAN HIS CAREER as a television writer-producer-director. Following that, he owned an advertising agency specializing in marketing supermarkets and was the creator, editor, and publisher of "In The Neighborhood," a local tabloid newspaper that promoted supermarkets and the communities in which they resided.

Eventually his passion turned to books and the web. He is a graphic designer, ghost writer, editor (eight books), and book designer with eight MarCom Awards, two Summit Awards, two Ippy Awards, and one Mom's Choice Award to his credit. He also has three MarCom awards for web design and a dozen Emmys as a television producer/director/writer. He was the director of the Cleveland Browns' "Masters of the Gridiron" (YouTube).

This is his fifth co-authoring project with Leslie Yerkes. The two have four more books in the works, with several more in the planning stages.

He serves on the board of directors for the Desoto Arts Council, The Hernando Veteran's Parade, and the Friends of the Von Theatre. In his spare time, he sings and plays guitar with Mississippi Greystone.

Randy is the owner of martinDESIGN.info.

"Hey, Buddha Bear. Can you see The Bridge?"

BRATENAHL OH 44108

Made in United States
North Haven, CT
22 June 2024

53946914R10061